SHANGHAI

KATHRYN WALKER

WORLD ALMANAC® LIBRARY

Please visit our web site at: www.worldalmanaclibrary.com
For a free color catalog describing World Almanac® Library's list of high-quality books and multimedia programs, call 1-800-848-2928 (USA) or 1-800-387-3178 (Canada). World Almanac® Library's fax: (414) 332-3567.

Library of Congress Cataloging-in-Publication Data

Walker, Kathryn.
Shanghai / by Kathryn Walker.
p. cm. — (Great cities of the world)
Includes bibliographical references and index.
ISBN 0-8368-5046-7 (lib. bdg.)
ISBN 0-8368-5206-0 (softcover)
1. Shanghai (China)—Juvenile literature. I. Title. II. Series.
DS796.S2W35 2005
951'.132—dc22 2004059415

First published in 2005 by
World Almanac® Library
330 West Olive Street, Suite 100
Milwaukee, WI 53212 USA

Produced by Discovery Books
Editors: Valerie Weber and Kathryn Walker
Series designers: Laurie Shock, Keith Williams
Designer and page production: Keith Williams
Photo researcher: Rachel Tisdale
Diagrams: Keith Williams
Maps: Stefan Chabluk
World Almanac® Library editorial direction: Mark J. Sachner
World Almanac® Library editor: Gini Holland
World Almanac® Library art direction: Tammy West
World Almanac® Library graphic design: Scott M. Krall
World Almanac® Library production: Jessica Morris

Photo credits: AKG Images, p. 10; Bettmann/Corbis: p. 16; Corbis, p. 14; Corbis/Freelance Consulting Services Pty Ltd: p. 23; Chris Fairclough Photography: cover and title page; Getty Images/The Image Bank: p. 17; Getty Images/AFP/Liu Jin: p. 22; Mary Evans Picture Library: p. 8; Panos/Mark Henley: pp. 26, 29, 30; Still Pictures/UM Photo Press International: pp. 4, 7, 9, 12, 21, 27, 31, 33, 35, 36, 37, 38, 40, 41, 42, 43; Still Pictures/Markus Dlouhy: p. 18; Still Pictures/Hartmut Schwarzbach: p. 32; Still Pictures/UM Photo Press Int.: p. 24; Trip: pp. 20, 28, 34.

Cover caption: Shanghai is one of China's top shopping centers, second only to Hong Kong. Sometimes known as the "golden mile," Nanjing Road has attracted tourists from all over China for many years and is said to be the busiest street in that country.

Printed in Canada

1 2 3 4 5 6 7 8 9 09 08 07 06 05

Contents

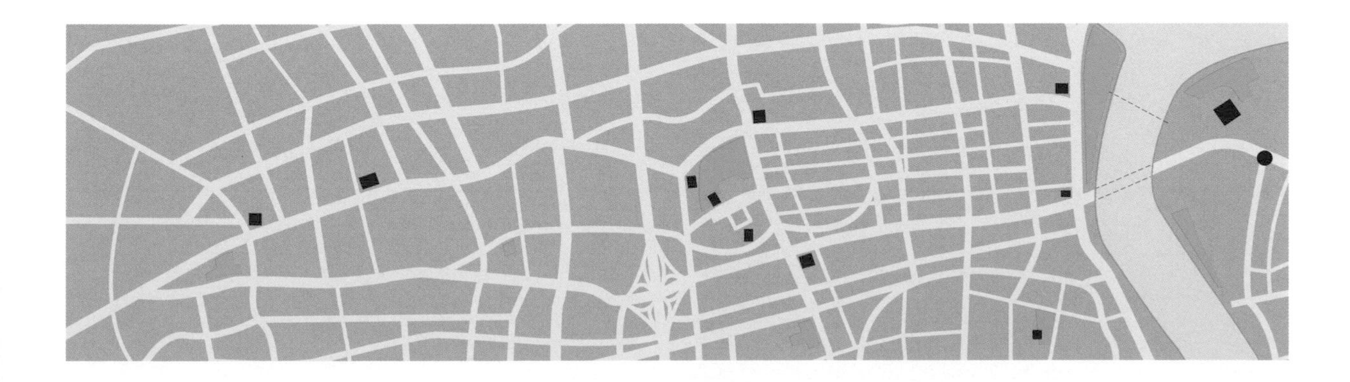

Introduction

Shanghai is a giant of a city—the largest in China—and one of the fastest developing cities in the world. It is the center of China's industry and commerce, with the largest and busiest port on the mainland. Shanghai is also one of the most wealthy and expensive cities in the country, while its people have a reputation for being smart, ambitious, and outward-looking trendsetters.

Rebirth

In the hundred years leading up to the Chinese Revolution of 1949, foreign settlements, also known as concessions, within the city dominated Shanghai. During

◄ *The skyscrapers of Shanghai's newly developed Pudong district face the old colonial buildings of the Bund across the Huangpu River.*

this period, it grew to be a world leader in trade and banking as well as a famously cosmopolitan city. After the revolution, it turned into the Cinderella of China—working hard to support the rest of the country but itself sadly neglected. In 1990, however, the central government announced plans to develop the city's Pudong area and allow foreign companies to invest in and begin businesses there.

Shanghai then embarked on a frenzy of building that has transformed the cityscape into a forest of skyscrapers and construction cranes. Elevated highways swoop through the city, and the world's fastest train glides though the brand-new Pudong district. Bold development projects are underway everywhere; the noise of drills and jackhammers fills the air.

CITY FACTS

Shanghai

Founded: 1292

Area (Municipal): 2,448 square miles (6,340 square kilometers)

Population (Municipal): 13,418,000

Population Density: 5,481 people per square mile (2,116 people per sq km)

(The population figure does not include temporary workers and unregistered migrants.)

Geography

Shanghai is located along the east coast of China within Jiangsu Province. The municipality (the city together with its suburbs and rural areas) is made up of eighteen districts and one county and includes approximately thirty islands. The county is Shanghai's largest island, Chongming, which lies in the Chang River (also known as the Yangtze). Mainland Shanghai is bordered on the north by the Chang, on the east by the East China Sea, and on the south by Huangzhou Bay. To the west lie Jiangsu and Zhejiang Provinces. Most of the municipal area is flat, a part of the Chang River delta plain, through which the Huangpu River winds before flowing into the mouth of the Chang north of the city.

"Over the decade it [the Shanghai Star] has charted the transformation of Shanghai from a third world backwater into the world's most dynamic metropolis. . . . Pudong has emerged out of swampy farmland to become one of the most spectacular cityscapes on Earth."

—The *Shanghai Star*, 2002.

City Layout

Within the city of Shanghai, the Huangpu River runs north to south, dividing it into two main areas—Puxi, which means "west

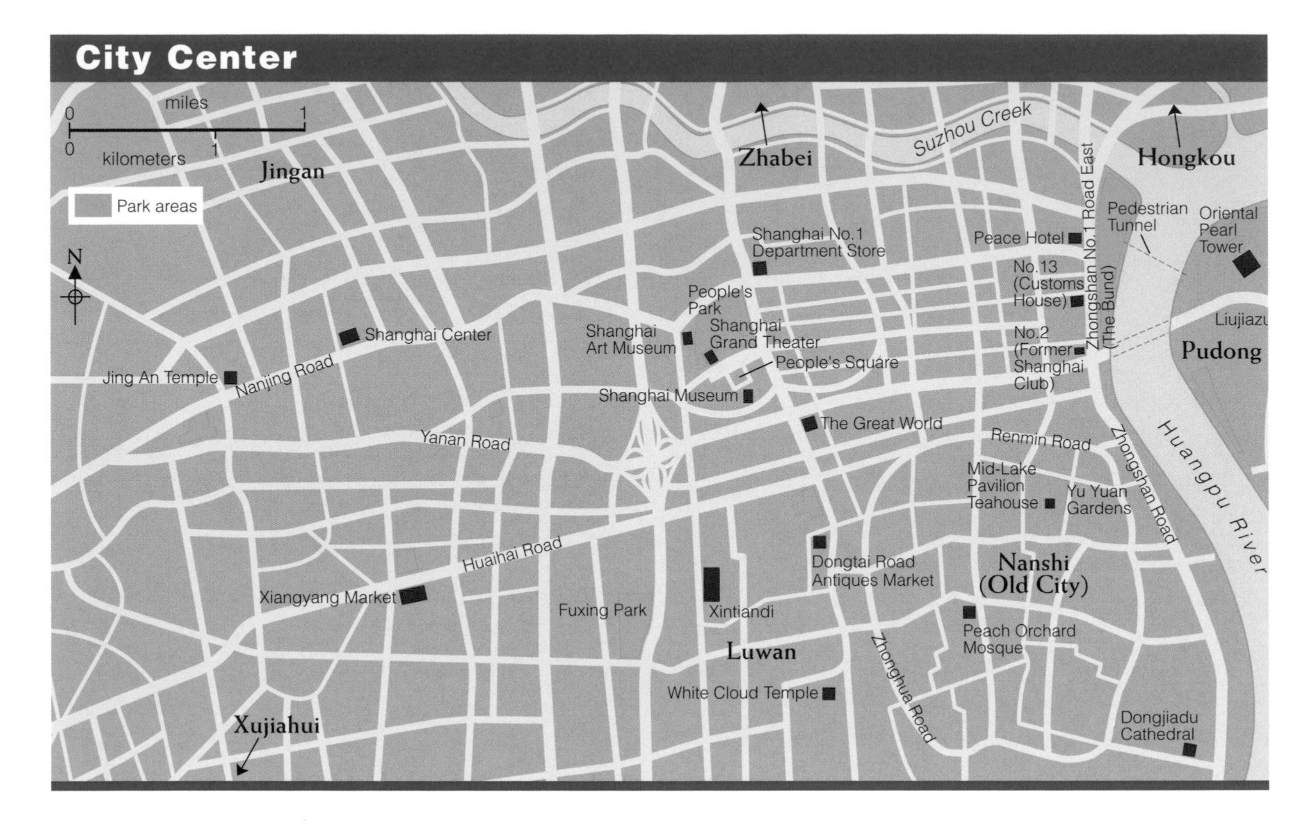

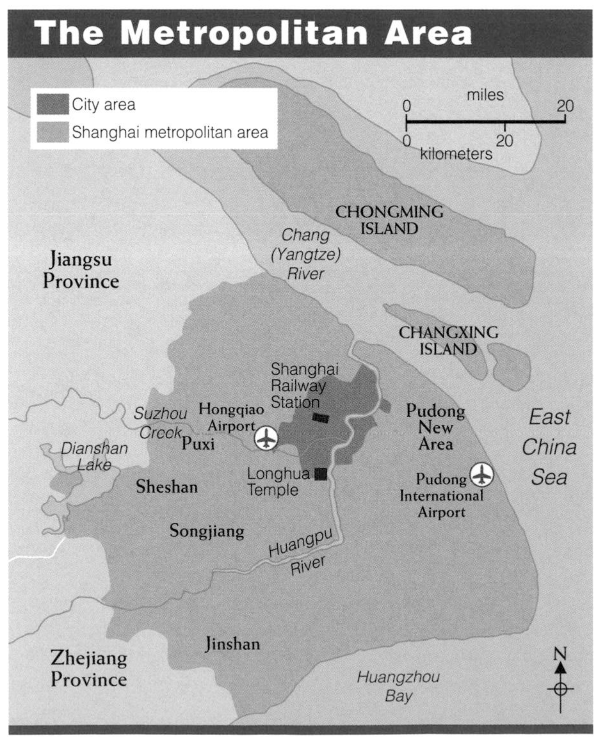

of the river," and Pudong, meaning "east of the river." Puxi is the older part of the city that once contained various foreign settlements and the original Chinese walled city. Pudong is a newly developed area and the ultramodern face of Shanghai.

Suzhou Creek runs roughly east to west through the city's center. The area south of Suzhou Creek up to Yanan Road once contained the original British settlement. Running through this section is Nanjing Road, one of the city's two top shopping streets. To the south of it and at the center of the city is People's Square.

A spectacular sweep of buildings dating from the late 1800s borders a waterfront stretch once named the Bund, but officially known today as Zhongshan No. 1 Road East. Its reputation as Shanghai's most famous sight is challenged by the space-age skyline of Pudong, which faces the former Bund across the Huangpu River. To the south is the site of the old Chinese city in the area of Nanshi, where Zhonghua and Renmin Roads trace the lines of the Old City's walls. Here, lanes and alleyways twist and turn in contrast with the gridlike streets elsewhere in Shanghai, while noisy markets and cooking smells from tightly packed lane houses keep alive the atmosphere of old China.

West of the Old City is the former French Concession area, centered around Fuxing Park and Shanghai's other main shopping street, Huaihai Road. Tree-lined streets with European-style buildings and bakeries still lend a French flavor to the area.

Climate

Shanghai has hot, humid summers and cold, dry winters. Moderate temperatures make spring and fall more comfortable seasons. Temperatures range on average between 77° Fahrenheit (25° Celsius) and 88° F (31° C) in July, which is typically the hottest month. The coldest is normally January, when temperatures average between 35° F (2° C) and 46° F (8° C). Typhoons can occur during July, August, and September but rarely cause serious damage. The rainy season lasts from May to September with the heaviest rainfall occurring between mid-June and early July, a period known as the Plum Rain because it coincides with the ripening of plums.

The Bund

An assortment of majestic, European-style buildings line a wide boulevard on the western bank of the Huangpu River, an area once known as the Bund (pictured here). *This 1 mile- (1.5 km-) stretch was originally a muddy waterfront that the foreign settlers had to fill in and embank, or construct a raised structure to hold back water, before buildings could go up. The name* Bund *comes from an Anglo-Indian word meaning "embankment." This was once the home of banks, trading houses, exclusive clubs, and hotels. Among its many notable buildings are the pyramid-topped Peace Hotel (originally the Cathay Hotel), the Customs House with its landmark clock tower, and No. 2, the former Shanghai Club that once boasted the world's longest bar. When the People's Republic of China (PRC) was established in 1949, the name* Bund*—an unwelcome reminder of days of Western domination—was changed to Zhongshan No. 1 Road East.*

CHAPTER 1

History of Shanghai

There is evidence that human settlements existed in the general area of Shanghai six thousand years ago, but it was not until the period when the Song dynasty ruled China (A.D. 960–1126) that the town of Shanghai emerged. By 1292, it had grown sufficiently for the Chinese government to create the county of Shanghai and make Shanghai itself the center of county government. In 1553, the people of Shanghai hurriedly built walls around the city to protect it from frequent raids by Japanese pirates. These walls encircled the original Chinese settlement, or Old City, until 1912, when, in the early years of the republic, the Chinese pulled them down.

Growth of the City

The main river that flowed through Shanghai used to be the Wusong (now Suzhou Creek), but its tendency to silt up made it difficult to navigate. The Huangpu was originally a minor waterway, but a combination of dredging, cutting channels, and building dikes gradually widened it. By

◀ *This drawing shows Shanghai in 1850, eight years after Britain defeated China in the First Opium War, forcing China to allow foreigners to trade with the city and live there.*

▲ *Within Shanghai's Old City stand the Yuyuan Gardens. Originally built in the sixteenth century, they are one of the last remnants of Shanghai's days before foreigners started to live in the city.*

the fifteenth century, it was Shanghai's major river. Boasting a reliable outlet to the East China Sea and the Chang (Yangtze) River, which ran deep into the silk- and tea-producing heart of China, Shanghai became an important port and trade center. Following the introduction of cotton to China in the thirteenth century, Shanghai rapidly developed into a center of cotton growing and cloth manufacturing.

Trade with the West

China had little interest in trade with foreign countries. Its economy was based on agriculture; the Chinese needed little of what foreigners had to offer so foreigners were not welcome. In 1760, the government restricted trade with Westerners to the port of Guangzhou (known in the West as Canton), south of Shanghai.

The British had a problem, however; they wanted silk and tea from China, and there was little they could trade in return. This imbalance meant that Britain was using an enormous amount of silver to buy these goods. In the early eighteenth century, the British began to trade the banned drug opium instead of silver. Opium is highly habit-forming, and, by the early

" . . . [The British] flag is become a pirate flag, to protect an infamous trade."

—William Gladstone, member of the British Parliament and later prime minister, 1840.

Shanghaied!

Since its early days as an international trading port, Shanghai was notorious as a place of vice, corruption, and violence. A little of that bad reputation lives on in the English language. When a ship was getting ready to leave the port, it was sometimes difficult to find enough men to crew the vessel. This lack led to the practice of forcing men to join the ships, often by drugging them, then carrying them off to the waiting vessels. Today, to shanghai *someone still refers to that practice but is also used in a broader sense to mean to force or trick someone into performing an unpleasant task.*

nineteenth century, millions of Chinese had become addicted to it. Despite a renewed ban on its import declared by Emperor Daoguang (of the Qing dynasty, which ruled China between 1644 and 1911), the British continued to smuggle huge amounts into the country. Silver flowed out of China in payment. In 1839, the Qing government took drastic action. Officials seized and destroyed thousands of chests of opium at Guangzhou and arrested British merchants.

▼ *Taken in the 1870s, this photo shows a Shanghai street scene with men pulling rickshaws—covered two-wheel carts with seating for one or two people.*

The Opium Wars

The incident at Guangzhou set off a war with Britain, later known as the First Opium War (1839–1842). The Chinese suffered a humiliating defeat and were forced to sign the Treaty of Nanking. Under its terms, five ports—including Guangzhou and Shanghai—were opened to unrestricted foreign trade and British residence. Further armed conflicts and treaties followed granting other countries, including the United States and France, similar rights.

The Settlements

In 1843, the British occupied an area north of the walled city and south of the Huangpu River. The French lived southwest of the British area in 1849, while the Americans settled in the Hongkou district north of Suzhou Creek in 1854. In 1863, the British and U.S. settlements, also known as concessions, merged to form the International Settlement. In 1895, the Japanese were granted a concession and became the largest non-Chinese group in Shanghai. The various groups of foreigners living within these zones were not subject to Chinese law.

Major European banks built branches in Shanghai, the city swelled with Chinese migrants and business executives, and trade prospered. By 1860, 25 percent of the shipping tonnage entering and departing China came through Shanghai. The foreigners built hospitals, churches, houses, and mansions; in the 1890s, they began establishing light industries such as textile manufacturing. A consul general appointed by Paris ran the French Concession, while the Shanghai Municipal Council governed the International Settlement.

The Taiping Rebellion

Floods and famines in mid-nineteenth century China, along with the weak government of the Qing dynasty, set the scene for the long and bloody Taiping Rebellion (1850–1864). A Christian convert, Hong Xiuquan, led the rebellion. He believed he was the brother of Jesus Christ and that it was his duty to overthrow the Qing dynasty to establish a more equal society for the Chinese. In 1853, a group called the Small Swords Society, which supported the Taiping rebels, took control of the Chinese walled city of Shanghai. They were finally driven out by a combination of imperial Chinese and French forces in 1855. In the meantime, the Americans, British, and French formed an army, called the Shanghai Volunteer Corps, to protect their settlements.

During the rebellion, thousands of Chinese fled to the safety of the settlements. Chinese had not been allowed to live in them before, but, with the prospect of money to be made, this rule quickly changed. Row upon row of houses were built to accommodate the newcomers, often sold or rented at unreasonably high prices to take advantage of the unstable political times.

▲ Built in the mid-nineteenth century, the Shanghai racecourse provided a place for wealthy foreigners to gather socially during the concession era.

"There are silk-winding mills so full of steam that the fingers of the mill-girls are white with fungus growths. If the children slacken in their work the overseers often plunge their elbows into the boiling water as a punishment. . . . In this city the gulf between society's two halves is too grossly wide for any bridge."

—Authors W. H. Auden and Christopher Isherwood, describing factories in *Hongkou, Journey to a War*, 1939.

Seeds of Rebellion

In 1911, the weakened Qing dynasty ended when the last emperor gave up the throne. Led by Sun Yat-sen, the Guomintang (Nationalist Party) declared China a republic. With no single faction strong enough to rule China, however, years of struggle between powerful regional warlords followed. A city of oppressed and exploited workers, Shanghai was a breeding ground for rebellion, and it was in the French Concession that the revolutionary Chinese Communist Party (CCP) held its first secret meeting in 1921.

In 1925, the Japanese manager of a mill killed a Chinese worker; an angry protest erupted. The Shanghai Municipal Police opened fire into the crowd, killing twelve Chinese in what became known as the "May 30 Atrocious Incident." Strikes followed, along with violent clashes between the Shanghai police and students and workers.

Best and Worst of Cities

By the 1920s and 1930s, Shanghai was famous as a center of entertainment, glamour, and sophistication. This reputation, together with many beautiful foreign buildings, earned it the title "the Paris of the East." Shanghai's nightclubs, cabarets, dance halls, racecourse, and world-famous clubs created a playground for wealthy Westerners, known as Shanghailanders. Because no passport was necessary to enter the city, it attracted many foreigners, some of them criminals and adventurers, some political refugees. Thousands of Russians escaping the Russian Revolution of 1917 made their way to Shanghai and were followed in the 1930s by Jews fleeing Nazi persecution in Europe. In the 1930s, the population reached 3 million, making Shanghai one of the world's largest cities at that time and one of its most cosmopolitan.

Green Gangsters

The Green Gang was a powerful Mafia-like society in Shanghai during the 1920s and 1930s. Its leader, Du Yuesheng, kept his base in the French Concession and controlled the city's opium trade along with gambling dens, protection rackets, smuggling, and other kinds of organized crime. "Big-Eared Du" worked closely with another Green Gang member, Huang Jinrong, known as "Pockmarked Huang," who was a senior Chinese officer in the French police. In spite of being a ruthless criminal, Du became a member of the French Concession's municipal council. Also, as reward for helping Jiang Jieshi suppress the Communists, he was appointed to the board of the Opium Suppression Bureau—a position that strengthened his grip on the opium trade. With dried monkey heads sewn to the back of his robe in the belief they would protect him from his many enemies, Du must have cut a frightening—and unmistakable—figure. He moved to Hong Kong in 1949 where he died, a multimillionaire, in 1951.

Meanwhile, Chinese workers in the Shanghai factories lived in desperate poverty and worked in dreadful conditions for very low wages. Slavery and child labor were common. The privileged life led by the wealthy foreigners stood in stark contrast with the life of the Chinese workers, which was hungry, hard, cruel, and usually short.

▲ *In 1937, Japanese troops invaded China, and in August of that year they attacked Shanghai. After a full-scale battle, they took control of the city.*

White Terror

Under the leadership of Jiang Jie-shi (previously known as Chiang Kai-shek), the Nationalists allied themselves with the Communists to try to unite the country, which at this point was deeply divided as rival warlords fought each other for control. In 1927, as the Nationalists marched on Shanghai, the Communists organized a strike in support of them that brought the city to a standstill. Jiang Jie-shi, however, chose this moment to bring this alliance to a sudden and violent end. With the help of Shanghai's Green Gang (see Green Gangsters, p. 13), the Nationalists shot thousands of striking workers and Communists in a surprise attack. In the weeks that followed, Communists in Shanghai were rounded up and either shot or beheaded in a period known as the "White Terror."

While blood ran in the Chinese city and suburbs, life continued more or less as usual in the settlements. In 1927, a new greyhound racetrack opened in the French Concession, while in 1929, the Shanghai millionaire, Victor Sassoon, proudly opened the Cathay Hotel (now the Peace Hotel) in the Bund; this art deco building was the height of elegance and modernity.

Japanese Occupation

In 1931, Japanese troops invaded Manchuria in northern China. In response, Shanghai boycotted goods from Japan. In January 1932, a clash between some Chinese and Japanese in Shanghai's Zhabei district gave Japan the excuse it wanted to attack the city. Japanese bombs destroyed Zhabei, killing more than ten thousand civilians. In 1937, a full-scale war broke out between Japan and China, and a hard and bloody battle followed in Shanghai. This time, there were foreign casualties as well, as bombs fell in the Bund and elsewhere in the concessions. Japanese troops took Shanghai, but at first, the concessions continued to govern themselves. Many foreigners left; those who stayed on lived in dangerous and violent times.

After Japan bombed the United States at Pearl Harbor, Hawaii, in 1941 in the early years of World War II, it seized control of the Shanghai's foreign settlements as well. In 1943, Japanese soldiers rounded up all Allied nationals in Shanghai (about eight thousand people) and put them in prison camps. That same year, Britain and the United States formally gave up their concessions in Shanghai, returning them to China. France surrendered its concession in 1946.

World War II ended in 1945; with Japan defeated, the Nationalists took control of the city once again. Some foreigners returned, and the city was soon back in business with the amount of foreign trade almost double what it had been before the war. Civil war raged in China as the Nationalists and Communists struggled for power.

The Communists Take Over

In 1949, Communist troops took control of Shanghai. On October 1 that year, their leader, Mao Zedong, declared the People's Republic of China (PRC). The Communists began the huge task of "cleaning up" the city—clearing slums, taking control of businesses, dealing with opium addicts, and ending practices such as child labor. The government turned the racecourse into a park for the people and used the stately Bund buildings as government offices.

The Cultural Revolution

In 1966, Mao Zedong chose Shanghai as the place to launch the Cultural Revolution, a radical movement aimed at destroying traditional Chinese culture and also at attacking Mao's political enemies. Thousands of young people became Red Guards, pledging to attack the four "olds:" old ideas, old culture, old customs, and old habits. Soon, as elsewhere in China, schools

▲ *Shanghai enthusiastically celebrated the founding of the People's Republic of China in 1949. Students on a truck carry portraits of Mao Zedong (right) and Zhu De, leader of the People's Liberation Army.*

were shut, teachers, intellectuals, and officials were persecuted or killed, and many were sent to the countryside for "reeducation" through hard labor. Any sign of Western influence was attacked; religion of any kind was outlawed. In Shanghai, revolutionary fervor and violence reached such a pitch that at one point the city ground to a halt and the army had to intervene.

During this period, Shanghai was the power base of the group—later known as the Gang of Four—that, along with Mao, masterminded the Cultural Revolution. The group included Mao's wife, Jiang Qing, who had once been a Shanghai movie actress. When Mao died in 1976, Jiang Qing tried to take control of the government, but she and the rest of the Gang of Four were arrested, brought to trial, and imprisoned.

▲ *Bold projects such as the Nanpu Bridge have created an exciting new cityscape for Shanghai.*

Shanghai Rising

After the Communist takeover, Shanghai continued to be a major port and industrial city. The money made in Shanghai, however, was used to develop other parts of China, while the city itself was neglected. When Deng Xiaoping came to power in 1978, he led China into a new era of reform, rebuilding the economy and opening it up again to the West.

During the 1990s, the city government invested huge amounts of money in a massive overhaul of its crumbling infrastructure. In 1990, China's central government designated Shanghai's Pudong district a Special Economic Zone—an area where special conditions would exist to encourage foreign and Chinese businesses to invest. As a result, many international companies made their Chinese headquarters there, and industrial output tripled in the 1990s. The city is still experiencing a massive building boom, and Shanghai has regained its cosmopolitan, outward-looking character.

CHAPTER 2

People of Shanghai

Shanghai is China's most populous city, with more than 13 million registered permanent residents. According to the Shanghai municipal government, however, if the total number of temporary residents and unregistered migrants are included, the population is closer to a staggering 20 million.

The increase in Shanghai's population over recent years is the result of people moving to the city from other parts of China, not of the number of children being born there. Every year since 1993, the city has reported a "negative natural growth rate" of its permanent residents, which means that more people are dying in Shanghai than are being born there.

The overwhelming majority of Shanghai's permanent residents (more than 99 percent) are Han Chinese. The Han group was an early Chinese dynasty that ruled the parts of China where the native Chinese originate. The remainder is made up of other ethnic groups, mainly the Hui, a Muslim minority; Manchus, who are

◀ *Banned for many years after the Revolution, ballroom dancing is now very popular with the Shanghainese; all around the city, people gather together in parks or on wide sidewalks to dance.*

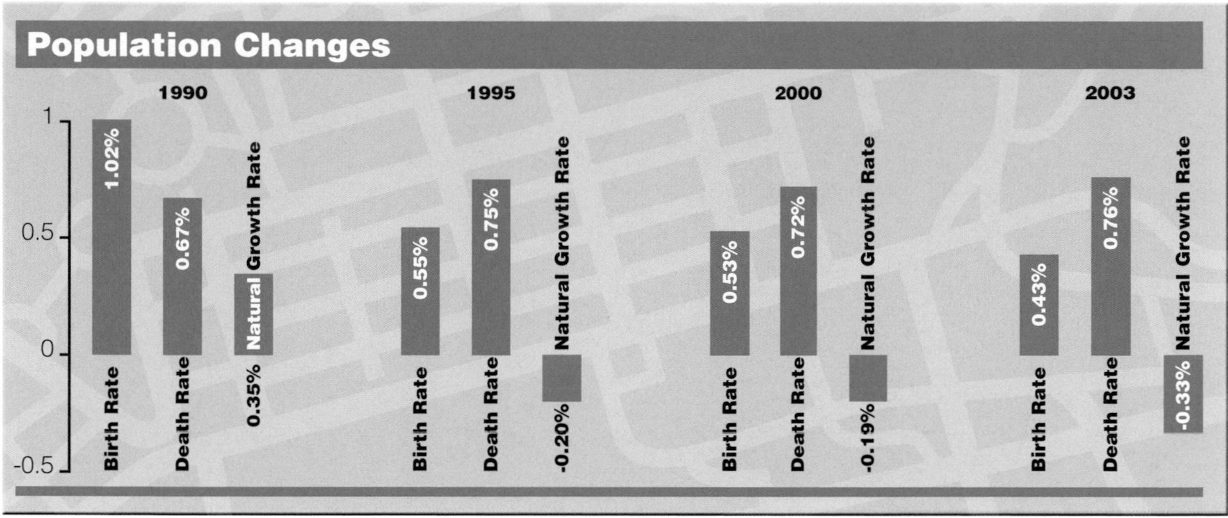

Source: Shanghai Municipal Government

Chinese originating from Manchuria; and Mongols, from an area north of China.

In addition, there are about 300,000 foreigners living in the city. The main language spoken in Shanghai is a regional dialcct callcd Shanghaincsc, which is vcry different from China's official language, Mandarin Chinese. Mandarin is used in street signs, newspapers, magazines, television, radio, and pop music. With the exception of the elderly, most Shanghainese can speak fluent Mandarin.

Religion

Officially, China is an atheist country—one whose people do not believe in the existence of a god. During the Cultural Revolution, all forms of religion were banned, and many places of worship were destroyed because the Communist government believed (and still does) that religion is a form of superstition that has been used in the past by

The Jews of Shanghai

Shanghai was once home to a thriving Jewish community. It included the wealthy Sasssoon, Hardoon, and Kadoorie families who made fortunes in Shanghai and built some of the city's finest colonial buildings. In the early twentieth century, Jews escaping persecution in Russia arrived in the city. The largest numbers of Jews (about twenty thousand), however, began arriving from Austria in 1938 to escape Nazi death camps. At that time, a visa was not needed to enter Shanghai, but Jews could only leave Austria if they had entry visas to another country. Many countries refused to grant visas, but Feng Shan Ho, the Chinese Consul General to Vienna, issued them to all those Jewish families who asked, ignoring orders from his superior to stop. In doing so, this quiet hero saved many thousands of lives.

騎般若之青獅乘三昧之白象

"I thought it only natural to feel compassion and to want to help. From the standpoint of humanity, that is the way it should be."

—Dr. Feng Shan Ho, former Chinese Consul General to Vienna from 1938 to 1940, on why he granted visas to many Jewish refugees, undated.

the ruling classes to keep the workers in their place. Since 1982, however, the Chinese people are again free to believe in any religion, but the state keeps religious practices under strict control. People can only worship in places approved by the government. The major religions allowed to practice in China are Taoism, Buddhism, Islam, Catholicism, and Protestantism. Many temples and churches in Shanghai have been restored and are now back in use.

▲ *Xujiahui Cathedral is a Catholic place of worship in southwest Shanghai, built in the early twentieth century in the European Gothic style of architecture.*

Traditional Beliefs

Traditional Chinese religion is based on three central philosophies or teachings: Taoism, Buddhism, and Confucianism. Taoism teaches people how to live in harmony with nature, while Buddhism teaches people how to achieve perfect happiness through overcoming their attachment to worldly things. Confucianism sets out a code of behavior that emphasizes the importance of family and respect toward elders and those in authority. Aspects of all three philosophies weave together in many Chinese people's beliefs.

◀ *These Buddhist monks are taking part in a ceremony at Shanghai's Longhua Temple.*

Places to Worship

The main religions practiced in Shanghai are Buddhism and Christianity. Among Shanghai's finest Buddhist temples are the Jing An Temple on the Nanjing Road, the Longhua Temple and Pagoda in southwestern Shanghai, and the popular Jade Buddha Temple in the Zhabei district, famous for its white jade Buddha statues.

Catholics can worship at Xujiahui Cathedral, also known as Saint Ignatius, a Gothic cathedral with soaring twin towers. There is also Sheshan Cathedral west of Shanghai and Dongjiadu Cathedral, the city's oldest Catholic church, in Nanshi. Protestants can worship at the redbrick Community Church south of Huaihai Road, founded by Americans in 1925. The Peach Orchard Mosque in the Old City serves Shanghai's Muslim community, while there are regular Taoist ceremonies in the nearby nineteenth-century White Cloud Temple.

Holidays and Celebrations

Shanghai loves to celebrate, and every month brings a festival of some description. Some are traditional Chinese festivals; others, such as the Shanghai International Arts Festival and the Tourism Festival, involve theater, music, and dance. Increasingly, Western celebrations are creeping into Shanghai's calendar, such as Halloween, Valentine's Day, and the Western calendar's New Year's Day.

The most important of the traditional festivals is the Spring Festival, also known as Chinese New Year. Celebrated in January or February, it marks the beginning of the lunar year with a week-long public vacation, elaborate meals, and fireworks; the best display is usually on Zhongshan Road. It is a time for visiting families and handing out red

◀ *Lanterns decorate the streets during the Lantern Festival that marks the end of Chinese New Year.*

envelopes containing money to children, unmarried relatives, and the elderly. It all ends on the fifteenth day of the lunar month with the Lantern Festival, when people carry lanterns through the streets and feast on sweet rice dumplings called *tangyuan*.

Everyone has a week's vacation again at the beginning of May to celebrate the workers of the world, and there is a one-day holiday on October 1 when National Day marks the founding of the People's Republic of China (PRC). The Mid-Autumn or Moon Festival is another well-loved traditional festival held in September or October, but it is not an official holiday. Like the Spring Festival, it revolves around family, and there is a delightful tradition of giving and eating round pastries with sweet or savory fillings called mooncakes.

▲ *Throughout China, teahouses are popular meeting places where a variety of teas are served. Shanghai's Old City is home to the Mid-Lake Pavilion Teahouse, a major tourist attraction. Its famous zigzag bridge was designed to prevent spirits from entering, as people believed spirits could not turn corners.*

▲ *In the Yuyuan Garden Bazaar in the Old City, people line up for the famously delicious snacks on sale at its street stalls.*

Dining Out

Shanghai has a fabulous variety of places to eat and these include some of China's most stylish restaurants. Apart from those serving traditional Shanghainese fare, there are plenty of restaurants specializing in other national and international cuisines as well as fusion food that mixes cooking styles from various countries. For the growing number of citizens who can afford to eat out, there is always a particular cuisine that is the latest fashion in Shanghai and a crop of new restaurants that cater to it.

Hot and Noisy

In Shanghai, eating out is a favorite social activity among family, friends, or work colleagues. Many business deals are also made over a restaurant table. Eating out is often a noisy event; the Shanghainese favor a busy and exciting atmosphere, described as renao, *literally meaning "hot and noisy."*

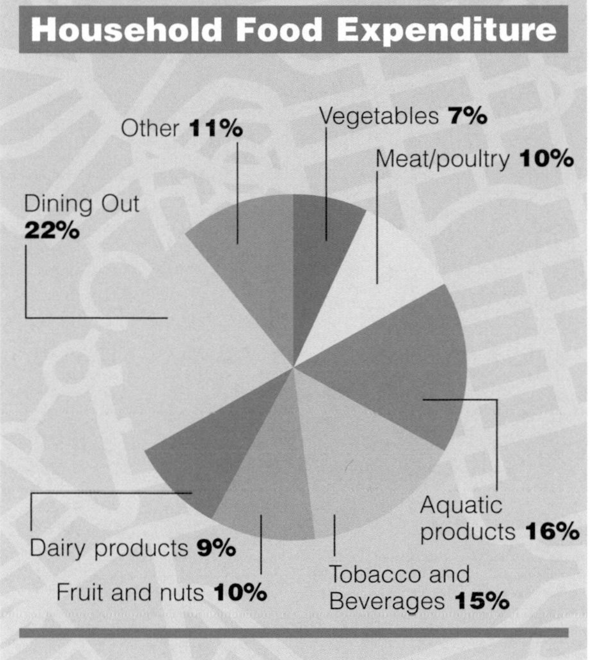

▲ *People in Shanghai spend more money per head on food than in any other province in China. This chart gives a breakdown of how the average urban household in Shanghai spends money on food.*

Shanghainese Cuisine

Huaiyang cuisine is a style of cooking particular to the area of eastern China that includes Shanghai, but the city has some of its own specialties and variations. Fish and seafood feature heavily, as do rich, sweetened sauces, while the freshness of ingredients used is considered very important. Rice, soup, and tea are served with most meals. Food is often "red-cooked"—prepared in a mixture of sugar and soy sauce—or marinated in Shaoxing wine. Otherwise, it can be fried in a variety of ways or steamed to keep its freshness. Shanghai chefs are also skilled at preparing vegetarian food that looks and tastes like meat dishes but uses soy bean products, vegetables, mushrooms, and bamboo shoots instead.

Fast Food

Everywhere in the city, shops and stalls sell all kinds of snack foods such as rice cakes, noodles, soups, dumplings, and the deep-fried dough sticks known as *youtiaou* that are a popular breakfast food. Shanghainese specialties include *xiaolongbao*, small and juicy meat-filled dumplings sold in bamboo steamer baskets, and *zhongzhi*, sticky rice mixed with meat and wrapped in a lotus leaf. Western fast-food chains such as McDonalds, Burger King, and KFC are also very popular in Shanghai.

Yangjingbang

Since the early days of the foreign concessions, the Shanghainese have had a reputation for their openness to Western culture. The word that has come to describe the resulting mixture of Chinese and Western influences in language, habits, or appearance is Yangjingbang. *This was the name of a creek that used to run north of the Old City. At the end of the nineteenth century, the creek was filled in to form a street (Yanan Road). The fact that this road was where Chinese and the British areas of Shanghai met is probably why the name has come to describe the Shanghainese's willingness to adopt Western ways.*

CHAPTER 3

Living in Shanghai

Shanghai has changed a great deal since the Communist government took control in 1949. The city's population grew rapidly during the 1950s, and to ease overcrowding in the city, the government built several new towns around Shanghai and large housing developments in the suburbs. As a result, many tens of thousands of city dwellers moved into the suburbs, easing overcrowding and making space for the new high-rise buildings that began to shape the Shanghai skyline in the 1990s. Often, this meant leaving primitive and overcrowded housing in the city for high-rise apartments with indoor plumbing and other modern amenities. The downside is that some people, mainly the elderly, feel isolated and miss the sense of community they had in the old neighborhoods.

To make better use of land and move more people out of the city, Shanghai has embarked on a new project to build nine new "satellite" towns. Each town will be built using the architectural styles of a particular country. A town in Jinshan district will have mainly two- or three-story buildings in North American style, while

◀ *Nanjing Road is one of Shanghai's top two shopping streets and home to some of the city's biggest department stores, including the No. 1 Department Store, a landmark dating from the 1930s.*

another in Songjiang district will recreate various British styles and include nine universities.

▲ *Shanghai has a growing number of vehicles on the streets; with more than one thousand bus lines, traffic congestion is a problem, particularly at rush hour.*

Traffic Congestion

In recent years, the city has tackled the problem of traffic congestion by investing huge amounts of money to build new bridges across the Huangpu and elevated highways, widen streets, and expand the subway system. The work has progressed at breakneck speed, but there are still times when the city gets congested. With more people able to afford cars and a growing population requiring more public transportation, the number of vehicles is increasing. The disruption caused by constant building work in the city also makes congestion worse.

In a controversial move, the city government has banned bicycles and other two-wheeled vehicles from the major streets in central Shanghai. As the bicycle is China's most common form of transportation and does not cause pollution, there has been an outcry. Officials have

Communal Living: Shikumen Longtangs

Unique to Shanghai is shikumen *(stone gate)* longtang *(lane housing), a nineteenth-century mixture of Western and Chinese architecture. Houses are connected to each other along straight lanes with an arch above the gateway to each lane. As Shanghai's population grew over the years, many houses were divided up so that several families occupied one house, sharing kitchens and bathrooms. In spite of such overcrowding, longtangs* (pictured here) *provide a safe environment and a strong sense of community for their occupants. About 45 percent of the city population still lives in longtangs. The more rundown ones are being demolished, while others are being modernized and restored.*

announced plans to build bicycle lanes, but many feel that the government should concentrate on reducing the number of cars instead.

Shopping Heaven

Although Hong Kong is China's top shopping center, Shanghai comes a close second. Its many department stores, slick shopping malls, and bustling markets stock a huge range of Chinese and imported goods. The main shopping streets are Huaihai Road and Nanjing Road, which is said to be the busiest street in China. New malls and stores are rapidly mushrooming all around the city to cater to the demands of the trendsetting, fashionable, and label-conscious Shanghainese with money to spend.

Markets and Stores

While prices in the shops are firm, customers can haggle or bargain over prices at Shanghai's markets. Dongtai Road Antiques Market, the biggest in the city, sells all kinds of antiques and curios, including some on which the paint has not yet had time to dry. Xiangyang Market in Huaihai Road sells copies of designer goods at bargain prices. The Nanshi area is home

▲ *Dongtai Road Antiques Market near Shanghai's Old City sells a wide variety of goods, including some genuine antiques along with reproductions and souvenirs.*

to the Dongjiadu Cloth Market, various antique markets, souvenir stalls, and craft shops. For a colorful and noisy experience, Shanghai has bird and flower markets where there are pets for sale such as rabbits, fish, and even caged crickets—prized by the Chinese for their chirping.

Up until 1990, people in Shanghai bought food either at "wet markets," where live chickens and seafood, newly killed animals, and freshly harvested vegetables are sold, or in food stores run by the government. Today, there are more than three thousand supermarkets, including some foreign chain stores, as well as many more small food stores throughout the city. Those who prefer to buy fresh food on a daily basis go to the "wet markets."

"Black July"

For students across China, the college entrance exams held in July are the most important exams of their lives. Competition for places at the top universities is fierce as families believe that students who gain entry to them stand the best chance of getting a top job. Parents often go to great lengths to help their children through this difficult time—staying up late with them as they study and sometimes booking them into hotels if they feel the students will study better there. These exams, always held in the heat of July, put the students under such pressure that the month has become known as "Black July." In Shanghai, construction workers are asked not to work at night around exam time so they do not disturb students.

Going to School in Shanghai

Starting at the age of six, children in China have to attend school for at least nine years. They study for six years at an elementary school, then go to a junior high school for three more years. They then choose whether or not to continue their education. Those who wish to continue need to pass entrance exams to senior high school or to midlevel technical schools. Those who move up into senior high school specialize either in science or the arts and prepare for the exams they must pass to enter college.

As part of its drive to make the city an international center of finance and trade,

▲ *At elementary schools, children learn about a wide range of subjects, including physical education, hygiene, music, and moral ethics.*

Shanghai is trying to encourage more of its population to become fluent in English. Schools are increasing their number of English classes, and some are trying out a bilingual teaching system where children are taught in English as well as Mandarin Chinese. In addition, high schools are beginning to recruit some overseas students and to send selected Chinese students to study abroad, with the aim of forging links with other countries.

Higher Education

Shanghai is a major center of higher education and scientific research. It has more than fifty institutes of higher

▲ *As more and more people, often from rural areas, move to Shanghai in search of better-paid work, the number of beggars and homeless people on the city streets increases.*

Sinking City?

Alarmingly, it seems that the ground that supports Shanghai is sinking at an average rate of 0.7 inches (1.5 centimeters) each year. Experts believe the cause is a combination of factors that include the weight of the city's new skyscrapers; in the 1960s, Shanghai had forty high-rises, but today there are more than three thousand. Another possible reason is that too much water has been taken out of the ground to supply the growing number of households. There have been warnings: In 2003, a pedestrian tunnel caved in, causing the collapse of an eight-story building, and in 2004, some stations on the light-rail train line closed because the ground was sinking around the tracks. The city government is carefully monitoring the situation and has restricted the amount of underground water usage, but there are plans for a further two thousand high-rises.

education, including major Chinese universities such as Fudan, Jiao Tong, Tongji, and East China Normal. There is a Shanghai branch of the Chinese Academy of Sciences where extensive scientific research is undertaken in cutting-edge technologies.

Too Many People

Shanghai's success story has brought its own problems, however. Incomes in Shanghai are the highest in China, and millions of migrants have moved into the city in search of better-paid work. The unemployment rate is rising while the municipal government struggles to create more jobs for the increasing population. The result is a growing number of beggars, a higher crime rate, and more homeless people. The gap between those who have money and those who do not is widening, and resentment is growing toward migrants, whom many Shanghainese blame for the increasing social problems in their city.

CHAPTER 4

Shanghai at Work

"To get rich is glorious."

—Deng Xiaoping, Chinese leader, 1982.

With a rapidly expanding economy, today's Shanghai is China's leading industrial and commercial center. Shanghai's population makes up just 1 percent of the Chinese nation, but in 2003, Shanghai accounted for more than 5 percent of the country's output, known as the Gross Domestic Product (GDP), and 13 percent of China's financial income. For more than twelve successive years, Shanghai's GDP has shown an increase of 10 percent or more. Since the 1990s, foreign money has been pouring into the city, and many foreign businesses have headquarters or industrial plants there. Today, companies owned by foreign investors produce over half the goods that Shanghai exports.

Key to Success

Shanghai's location at the mouth of the Chang (Yangtze) River and also on the East China Sea has been vital to the city's success. The city has the third largest port in the world; in 2003, about 25 percent of China's total exports passed through Shanghai.

◀ *A man works on the production line of Volkswagen Shanghai, a joint business venture between the German car manufacturer Volkswagen and the Shanghai Automotive Industry Corporation.*

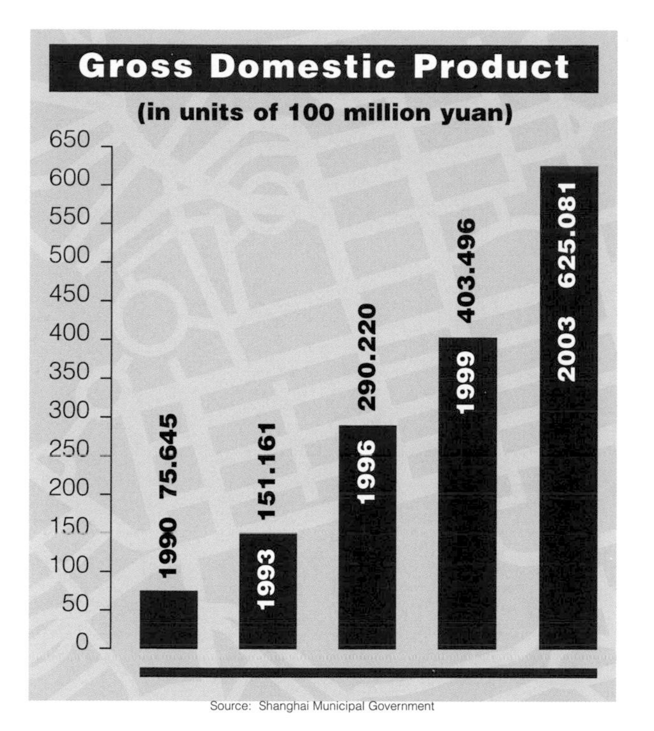

▼ *Shanghai's unique location is ideal for shipping goods into and out of China's interior, making it one of the world's busiest ports.*

Its good rail and road networks make it easy to import raw materials for industry, distribute goods, and for the city to serve as a gateway to the industrial centers and cities of the interior. Another key to the city's success is its highly skilled and productive workforce, while the willingness of the Shanghainese to adapt to Western ways helps attract foreign investors.

Industrial Strengths

Shanghai is one of China's top producers of iron, steel, and automobiles. Other important industries include chemicals and petrochemicals, electronics, power, telecommunications, machinery, electrical appliances, textiles, and shipbuilding. High-technology industries are growing in strength. About half the workforce is employed in the manufacturing industry. Shanghai is also becoming an important center for banking and has its own stock exchange.

The service industries—industries providing people with a service rather than a product, such as telecommunications, finance, and retail—now account for more than half of Shanghai's GDP. Supplying the needs and demands of such a large and relatively wealthy population, along with those of a growing number of tourists, means many business opportunities. While a large number of Shanghainese cannot afford luxury goods, there are enough wealthy and fashion-conscious citizens and tourists to create a big demand for elegant shopping malls with expensive designer outlets.

Pudong

Before 1990, Pudong was mostly marshy farmland on the eastern bank of the Huangpu River. The government then decided to develop the area as a Special Economic Zone, creating an environment that would attract foreign investment. Across the river from the former Bund lies Pudong's Liujiazui financial and trade zone, where national and international banks and financial institutions have headquarters. With its gleaming skyscrapers, Liujiazui looks like something from a science fiction movie. It isn't all work in Pudong though; there are shopping malls, museums, theaters, housing developments, Shanghai's largest park, and even a safari park. Nevertheless, the Puxi area wins hands down when it comes to nightlife.

Pollution

With many factories and oil refineries—and with coal a major fuel for industries and homes—it is no surprise that Shanghai suffers from air pollution. The vast quantities of industrial and human untreated waste pumped out into the Huangpu River are causing water pollution and problems in the water supply—as well as a terrible smell.

Noise pollution is also a big problem, partly from heavy traffic but also from the constant noise of construction work. The city government is determined to cure these problems, however. As part of a drive to improve the city's environment, a number of sewage-treatment plants are under construction. In addition, taxis have been converted to run on natural gas to cut down emissions, and there are plans to ban noisy powerboats from the main waterways.

Government

Shanghai lies within Jiangsu Province but is one of China's four independent municipalities, which means that China's central government controls the city instead of the provincial government. Shanghai's governing body is the Shanghai People's Congress, which is controlled by the Chinese Communist Party. Voters elect district and county representatives to Congress, but the Communist Party controls the appointment of senior positions such as mayor. The Shanghai Municipal Government is made up of various departments that are answerable to the People's Congress. Between them, they are responsible for the day-to-day running of the city.

The mayor of Shanghai is an important political office. Previous mayors, such as Jiang Zemin and Zhu Rongji, have gone on to hold top positions within China's central government. It was when they led the government—during the 1990s, Jiang Zemin was state president as well as leader of the Communist Party and Zhu Rongji was premier—that Shanghai was put forward as the city that would lead China's economic development. Mayor Han Zheng took office in 2003.

▲ *Appointed mayor of Shanghai in 2003, Han Zheng is a native of Zhejiang Province and a senior economist.*

Planes, Boats, and Trains

Shanghai is a major transportation hub. Two airports serve the city: Pudong Airport about 19 miles (30 km) southeast of Shanghai, and Hongqiao Airport about 11 miles (18 km) southwest of the city's center. The majority of international flights are routed through the newer Pudong Airport, while Hongqiao receives the bulk of flights within the country.

Being both a sea and river port, Shanghai is a center for ocean going and Chang River shipping and passenger boats traveling to

▲ *The subway system is often the fastest way of getting around the city, but during rush hours, the platforms get terribly overcrowded.*

international destinations as well as places within China. Hong Kong is a three-day boat journey away and Osaka in Japan about a two-day trip. Shanghai's main railroad station is the Shanghai Railway Station in Zhabei District, while some trains run to stations in the city's northwest and southwest. Services are efficient, and there is an extensive railroad network.

Getting around the City

Shanghai's bus service is cheap and extensive, but, like all forms of transportation in the city, it gets extremely crowded during rush hours. Not for the fainthearted, it is then a case of push, shove, and hang on tight. Bus drivers are known to break speed limits and ignore red lights so the traffic authority has installed boxes in some buses that record the drivers' performance, including traveling speeds. Metered taxis are plentiful in Shanghai and not very expensive.

The subway offers a clean and efficient way of getting around the city that is easy to use. Opened in 1995, it currently consists of two underground lines: Line 1 runs north and south, while Line 2 runs east and west and will eventually link Shanghai's two airports. The lines meet at People's Square in the geographical center of Shanghai, the city's busiest station. Line 3 is the Pearl Mass Transit Light Rail, which runs mainly above ground. It links the south with the north of the city, passing through the western outskirts. If construction goes according to city plans, Shanghai will have eleven subway lines and ten light-rail lines by 2025.

MagLev

In keeping with the futuristic image of new Shanghai, the MagLev train (pictured here) *is the first magnetic levitation system to be put to into commercial use. Powerful magnets allow the train to rise less than half an inch (10 millimeters) above the track, making the journey smooth and quiet. The train links Pudong Airport to Longyang Lu Subway Station in Pudong, a distance of 19 miles (30 km). This journey takes just eight minutes on a train capable of a maximum speed of about 270 miles (430 km) per hour.*

CHAPTER 5

Shanghai at Play

Shanghai is a fun-loving city with a vibrant nightlife and cultural scene. At night, Puxi buzzes with bars, pubs, bowling alleys, karaoke bars, and nightclubs that range from sleek to seedy. One of the hottest nighttime spots is Xintiandi, a neighborhood where old shikumen longtang housing has been redeveloped into an entertainment district. The project has been so successful that it seems likely to set the style for similar projects in the city.

Music

Rock bands play at a variety of clubs and bars in the city, while big-name international and Chinese pop stars play at the Shanghai Stadium. Jazz has been popular in Shanghai since the 1920s and can be heard at bars, clubs, and elegant hotels around the city. Western and Chinese classical music and opera are performed at various venues in the city. Chinese opera is very different from the Western variety; it combines song in the Chinese musical style with dance, mime, and acrobatics together with highly stylized movements, heavy makeup, and brilliant costumes.

The spectacular Shanghai Grand Theatre at People's Square is a modern glass complex

◄ *Shanghai's top soccer team, the Shenhua Blue Devils, has a devoted following of fans; matches draw big crowds to their home stadium in Hongkou.*

that has become a glittering landmark and a world-class venue for music, ballet, opera, and drama. Another landmark, the 1930s Shanghai Concert Hall, has been recently relocated to Yanan Road. This fine building was actually moved two blocks from its original location, very slowly, on sliding rails—a journey that took twelve days to complete.

Acrobatics and Dance

Acrobatics is a traditional Chinese art form dating back more than two thousand years and one that the Communist government has always approved of. The Shanghai Acrobatics Troupe is one of the best in the world and can be seen most nights at the Shanghai Center Theater, part of the Shanghai Center complex on Nanjing Road. Performances combine beautiful costumes, comedy, and magic with breathtaking stunts. Classical ballet is performed in the city as well as a unique Chinese blend that involves elements of Chinese opera.

Movies and Theater

The government sees drama as a way of promoting powerful political and cultural messages, so it controls which plays are performed in the city. It also decides which movies can be shown. The majority of films released are Chinese-made, but some foreign films are also screened, including a limited number of Hollywood movies. The Shanghai International Film Festival held in June is a popular event that brings more foreign films to the city.

The Great World

The Great World near People's Square is a 1920s building with a tiered tower like a wedding cake. It opened as a multistory entertainment complex but became somewhat seedier in the 1930s when gangster "Pockmarked Huang" took it over and added gambling dens, a shooting gallery, fortune-tellers, earwax extractors—you name it. One visitor reported being shown an "open space" at the top of the building where those who had gambled away their fortunes were very welcome to throw themselves to their deaths. Today, the Great World offers a little bit of everything—opera, acrobatics, films, a ghost train, and more—to amuse all age groups.

Galleries and Museums

At People's Square, a striking modern building houses the Shanghai Museum, where collections of bronzes, ceramics, jade, paintings, and calligraphy trace four thousand years of Chinese culture. Nearby, the 1930s British racecourse building is now the Shanghai Art Museum exhibiting contemporary painting and sculpture. Over in Pudong, the basement of the futuristic Oriental Pearl Tower contains the Shanghai Municipal Historical Museum, where visitors can see what life in old Shanghai

▲ *The unusual design of the state-of-the-art Shanghai Museum is based on the form of an ancient bronze cooking vessel called a* ding.

was like. The Shanghai Science and Technology Museum is another impressive modern building with an indoor rainforest, earthquake simulator, and an interactive section for children.

Sports

Soccer is now the top spectator sport in Shanghai. The thirty-five-thousand-seat Hongkou Stadium north of the city is home to the city's premier soccer team and one of China's best, the Shenhua Blue Devils. Basketball also has a strong following, and Shanghai's team, the Shanghai Sharks, play at Luwan Stadium. Their star player was 7 foot 5-inch (2.26-meters) Yao Ming, now with the National Basketball Association's (NBA's) Houston Rockets and sometimes referred to as "the Great Wall of China."

China's first international auto-racing circuit opened in Shanghai in June 2004 and hosted the first Chinese Formula One Grand Prix in September 2004. Each September, the Shanghai Open Tennis Championship attracts top international stars to the city. Shanghai was also selected as the host for the Tennis Masters Cup for the period 2005 to 2007 to be held at the Qizhong Tennis Center, which is currently under construction.

Popular participation sports in Shanghai include table tennis, tennis, badminton, and bowling. Many of the wealthier Shanghainese join gyms or fitness clubs, while golf is a very expensive sport and a favorite with the wealthy business elite.

▲ *Dating from the Ming dynasty of 1368 to 1644, the beautiful classical gardens of Suzhou are now a World Heritage Site and a famous Chinese attraction.*

City Retreats

New buildings in Shanghai continue to appear at mind-boggling rate, but thankfully, the number of green spaces has also increased in recent years. Locals often take their pet birds in their cages out for walks in the parks or go there to fly kites with their children. Particularly in the early mornings before going to work, people gather in the city parks and on wide sidewalks to practice *tai chi*, aerobics, or pair up for some ballroom dancing.

Excursions

There are several interesting daytrip destinations for a change from the fast pace of Shanghai life. Dianshan Lake, 40 miles (64 km) southwest of Shanghai, has recreational facilities such as a water-sports park and a golf course. The Grand View Garden near the lake recreates the one featured in the popular Chinese novel *Dream of Red Mansions*; actors play out scenes from the book in the garden buildings.

Moving farther afield, Suzhou, 50 miles (80 km) northwest of Shanghai, has a historic center with canals and bridges that make it one of China's most beautiful towns. It is famous for its exquisite classical Chinese gardens. Possibly the best antidote to the noise of Shanghai is the island of Putuoshan, about 155 miles (250 km) south of the city and a ferry trip away. It is a peaceful island, dotted with temples, monasteries, pagodas, and fringed with sandy beaches.

Looking Forward

"Better City, Better Life."

—Theme of the 2010 World Expo.

In 2002, Shanghai celebrated winning its bid to host the 2010 World Expo. Aiming to promote trade, this event allows countries to present their arts, crafts, inventions, and industrial products. It is a golden opportunity for China to impress and make itself better known to the world, while Shanghai will get the chance to show off its dazzling new image and, hopefully, boost its economy. In preparation, the city is speeding up plans to improve its environment, transportation, and public services. Shanghai is determined to make it a memorable World Expo.

Investing in the Future

Shanghai has many other new projects planned. They include redeveloping 53 miles (85 km) of the Huangpu riverbank to create homes, offices, and entertainment facilities, together with green spaces and the Expo village. In 2007, a new dock for cruise ships will open that could bring in a million more visitors each year. Work is also underway on a new deep-water port that will be able to handle more than 30 million

◀ *Within the last decade the Shanghai cityscape has changed with astonishing speed, particularly in Pudong, shown here. With ambitious new projects planned, there are no signs of the pace slackening.*

Chongming Island

Chongming Island, the third largest island in China, lies in the middle of the Chang River and makes up one-sixth of Shanghai's total land area. Today, it is accessible from Shanghai only by ferry, but that will soon change. A 5.5 mile- (9 km-) long tunnel under the Chang will connect Pudong with neighboring Changxing Island; then an elevated highway across Changxing will link with a bridge across the river to Chongming. The plan is to develop the island in an environmentally friendly way, protecting its wetlands nature reserve and increasing its forest park recreational area. Pollution-free industries, stadiums, homes, hotels, and offices are planned. The result should be a major tourist attraction, especially if plans for a theme park such as Disneyland become reality.

▲ *The banners in this street scene celebrate Shanghai winning its bid to host the 2010 World Expo and bear the message "Bring Our Wishes into Reality."*

containers each year. The list goes on—Shanghai has no plans for slowing down.

The Cost of Change

This relentless development brings its own problems. The government is efficiently tackling the overcrowding, pollution, heavy traffic, and power shortages, but there are other issues. As Shanghai is forced to compete with international businesses, many of its homegrown enterprises fight for survival. Some state-run industries, whose main purpose in the past was to provide just for China, employ too many people and are proving unprofitable. As businesses close down or reduce staff numbers, the resulting unemployment widens the gap between the haves and have-nots—something that runs against Communism's basic principle of equality. Corruption is also a problem; laws that relate to business are not yet properly in place in mainland China, and new offices in Pudong stand empty as a result.

The city is quickly building a framework for a world-class city, but there is still a way to go before it realizes its huge ambitions. In the meantime, Shanghai is working on it—at full speed ahead.

Time Line

1292 The Yuan imperial government creates the county of Shanghai and makes Shanghai the center of county government.

1553 A wall is built around the main area of Shanghai to protect it from pirate raids.

1839–1842 The First Opium War is fought between China and Britain. The Treaty of Nanjing is signed, opening five ports, including Shanghai, to foreign trade.

1843–1854 The British, French, and Americans establish concessions in Shanghai.

1850–1864 The Taiping Rebellion rages throughout China, resulting in an influx of Chinese refugees to the settlements.

1853–1855 The Small Sword Society, a branch of the Taipings, takes control of the Chinese walled city.

1863 The American and British settlements merge to form the International Settlement.

1895 The Japanese establish a settlement.

1911 The last Qing emperor steps down; the Nationalist Party under the leadership of Sun Yat-sen declares a republic.

1921 The first meeting of the Chinese Communist Party (CCP) is held in Shanghai.

1925 A Chinese worker is killed by a Japanese mill manager; during the protests that follow, the Shanghai Municipal Police shoot twelve Chinese.

1927 The Nationalists, led by Jiang Jie-shi, march on Shanghai; they then launch a surprise attack on their allies, the CCP, killing strikers and Communists.

1931 Japanese troops invade Manchuria.

1932 Following a clash between Chinese and Japanese in Shanghai, Japan bombs the Zhabei district.

1937 Full-scale war breaks out between China and Japan; Japanese troops take Shanghai.

1941 Japan seizes control of Shanghai's foreign settlements.

1943 Japan puts all Allied nationals into prison camps; later that year, Great Britain and the United States formally give up their concessions.

1945 World War II ends, and Japan is defeated; Nationalists again take control of Shanghai; civil war rages as Nationalists and Communists fight each other.

1949 In May, the Communists take control of Shanghai; in October, the leader of the Communists, Mao Zedong, declares the People's Republic of China.

1966–1976 The Cultural Revolution takes place, masterminded by Mao together with the "Gang of Four" based in Shanghai.

1976 Mao dies; the Gang of Four is arrested.

1978 Deng Xiaoping, China's new leader, leads a period of economic reform.

1990 Shanghai's Pudong area is established as a Special Economic Zone, triggering a new era of development for the city.

2002 Shanghai wins its bid to host the 2010 World Expo.

Glossary

Allied nationals people who originally came from the Allied nations united to fight in World War II, including the United States, Great Britain, the Soviet Union, and China.

boycotted refused to buy from or deal in a commercial way with a country or organization as a form of protest.

Buddhism a world religion founded by Siddhartha Gautama (c.563–c.483 B.C.), known as the Buddha; Buddhists believe in rebirth and that people's deeds during their life influence their successive lives.

civil war war between people of the same country.

commerce buying and selling goods on a large scale, between countries, cities, or individuals.

Communism a system of government that aims to create a classless society where everyone is equal; businesses are run by the state for the good of the people, and all property is communally owned.

concession land granted by the Chinese government to foreign powers.

Confucianism a philosophy based on the teachings of Confucius, the Latin name of K'ung Fu-tse, who lived in China about 400 B.C.; Confucian thought stresses the importance of family and social ties and respect for authority.

congestion clogging up or overcrowding.

containers large, box-car like receptacles of a standard size used for transporting goods.

controversial causing strong disagreement or discussion.

cosmopolitan having experience of other countries and cultures; not tied by the limitations of one country.

dynasty a family that rules a country for several generations.

economy a country's finances, industry, and services.

elite a small, privileged group of people.

exploited taken advantage of or made use of in an unfair manner.

Gross Domestic Product (GDP) a way of assessing economic performance by adding up the total value of all the goods and services produced within a country or region during a given period (usually a year).

infrastructure the system of public works, such as water, roads, and electricity, in a region.

investment putting money to a particular use to make a profit.

lane houses residences that are attached together along a narrow road.

migrants people who move from one part of the country to another or from one country to another.

Nationalists members of the Chinese Nationalist Party (also known as the Guomintang), founded by Sun Yat-sen in 1919; the Nationalists fought the Communists for control of China, but lost.

opium an addictive narcotic drug made from poppies.

oppressed treated unjustly or cruelly.

passport a formal document issued by a country that allows a person to travel to another country and return legally.

raw materials substances out of which products are made.

republic a form of government in which authority belongs to the people, who elect representatives to make laws and manage the government.

retail the sale of goods to the public.

smuggle to bring in or take out of a country illegally and secretly.

strikes when workers refuse to work because of a dispute or in protest.

suppress to put down or crush.

Taosim a Chinese religion; Tao means the "way," and its founder Lao-tzu, is said to have lived during the sixth century B.C.

trade buying and selling.

venues places where special events are held.

visa an official written permission given by a country; attached to a passport, it allows a person to enter and travel within a country.

Further Information

Books

Hatt, Christine. *Mao Zedong (Judge for Yourself)*. World Almanac Library, 2003.

Hoobler, Thomas, and Dorothy Hoobler. *Confucianism (World Religions)*. Facts on File, 2004.

Knowles, Christopher. *Fodor's Citypack Shanghai (Citypack)*. Fodor's Travel Publications, 1999.

Malaspina, Ann. *The Chinese Revolution and Mao Zedong in World History (In World History)*. Enslow Publishers, 2004.

Thich Nhat Hanh. *A Pebble for Your Pocket*. Parallax Press, 2002.

Wilkinson, Philip. *Buddhism (Eyewitness Books)*. DK Publishing, 2003

Web sites

www.educ.uvic.ca/faculty/mroth/438/CHINA/chinese_new_year.html
You can find out about the customs, foods, and beliefs surrounding Chinese New Year on this site.

library.thinkquest.org/26469/index2.html
Find out about Chinese cities and historical figures such as Jiang Jie-shi on this Web site .

www.shanghai-window.com/shanghai/tourism/yuyuan/yuyuan.html
You can see pictures of the famous Yuyuan Gardens of southeastern Shanghai on this Web site.

www.shanghai-window.com/shanghai/zoo
Learn about rare and unusual animals when visiting the links on the Shanghai Zoological Park web site.

www.wsu.edu:8080/~dee/CHING/OPIUM.HTM
This site gives a detailed history of the Chinese and British dispute over the opium trade.

Index

Page numbers in **bold** indicate pictures.